S0-ARI-002

GO FOR THE GOLD

Eric Harvey

How to achieve meaningful and lasting **success**

GO FOR THE GOLD

Eric Harvey

How to achieve meaningful and lasting **success**

To order additional copies of this book, or for information about other WALK THE TALK® products and services, contact us at **1.888.822.9255** or visit **www.walkthetalk.com**.

GO FOR THE GOLD © The WALK THE TALK® Company

No part of this book may be reproduced in any form without written permission from the publisher. International rights and foreign translations are available only through negotiation of a licensing agreement with the publisher. Inquiries regarding permission for use of the material contained in this book should be addressed to: The WALK THE TALK Company, 1100 Parker Square, Suite 250, Flower Mound, TX 75028, 972.899.8300

WALK THE TALK books may be purchased for educational, business, or sales promotion use. WALK THE TALK®, The WALK THE TALK® Company, and walkthetalk.com® are registered trademarks of Performance Systems Corporation.

Printed in the United States of America

10 9 8 7 6 5 4 3 2 1

For everyone
who seeks
SUCCESS

GO FOR THE GOLD

INTRODUCTION

The foundation of this book for me began many years ago when I was being discharged from the military. I had served in Army Air Defense and was about to be released – and return to college to finish my degree. In a final transition meeting with my commanding officer, he told me how proud he was of my service (which meant a lot to me) and then he asked me some simple, yet extremely profound questions about my life plans.

The conversation went something like this:

Him: So ... what are you looking for in life?

Me: To be happy and successful.

Him: And what does happiness and success mean to you?

Me: Have a good job and a great career.

Him: Is that it?

Me: No ... I want a successful personal life as well.

Him: So, what will it take to make that happen?

Me: A lot of hard work and a little luck.

Him: **IS THAT ALL?**

His last question stumped me a bit. I'm not even sure how I answered it that day, but I do clearly remember that it got me really thinking and wondering …

What *does* it take to achieve meaningful and lasting success?

For the past thirty-plus years of my professional life, I've had the good fortune of working with hundreds of organizations, worldwide, and the thousands of people who comprise them – ranging from the "horribles" to the "best of the best." I've also studied politicians, sports icons, famous public figures, as well as personal friends and colleagues. Not everyone, of course, but many of those I've studied have achieved meaningful success, are admired, and have become role models for us all.

So what did I learn from a lifetime of observation and analysis? Two primary lessons which have been profound for me and hopefully will prove invaluable for you:

1

**Success isn't determined by
who you are;
it's built by what you DO.**

And

2

**All truly successful people DO
the same things:**

They SHOW UP,

They SUIT UP,

They "GO FOR THE GOLD."

Explaining and examining those behaviors – the *action* components of success – is what GO FOR THE GOLD is all about.

As you read, you'll examine the importance of **Showing Up** and always "being there" – in each moment you have and for every situation you face.

You'll understand the importance of **Suiting Up** for success and being ready to take advantage of every opportunity you are presented with.

And then you'll discover the true meaning of "**Gold**" – how it relates to all aspects of your professional and personal life, and how you can attain success for yourself and others.

My hope is that the messages in this book are both inspiring and guiding for you and others. Please accept them, absorb them and, most importantly, APPLY them, and they will lead you to higher levels of happiness and achievement.

I've discovered that meaningful and lasting success is neither elusive nor fleeting – it's available and it's fully attainable.

Your GOLD is out there waiting for you to discover it and enjoy all the "riches" it brings. All you need is a treasure map to guide you on this journey.

This is your map!

Let the journey begin.

Stop dreaming and
start DOING

Wherever you are, whenever the time, whatever the circumstances, **you must be ...**

PHYSICALLY PRESENT

MENTALLY FOCUSED

EMOTIONALLY COMMITTED

If you don't fully show up, neither will success.

Eighty percent of success is showing up.

~ Woody Allen

Have you ever experienced situations in which people are there, but they're not really *there* – where they are AT a place but not really IN the moment?

The players were on the field, but our team didn't show up!

Of course you have! We all have! And we quickly learned that while physical presence is obviously necessary to be "in the game," it alone is not enough to make us successful.

If our heads and hearts aren't there as well, our bodies are merely occupying space, and we're primed to squander any opportunities that come our way ... to pass over the things that are truly important:

Our Work, Our Families, Our Friends, Our Colleagues, and Our Communities

Fact is ...

If you arrive at work with the intention of just getting through the day,

YOU HAVEN'T SHOWN UP!

If you're "multitasking" during a business meeting rather than paying full attention and contributing,

YOU HAVEN'T SHOWN UP!

If you fail to truly listen to someone because you're preoccupied with your own thoughts and priorities,

YOU HAVEN'T SHOWN UP!

If you're at your child's school event but you're focused on texting friends,

YOU HAVEN'T SHOWN UP!

If "family time" means watching a ball game that no one else cares about,

YOU HAVEN'T SHOWN UP!

If you avoid helping a colleague in need because you "don't have the time,"

YOU HAVEN'T SHOWN UP!

If you fail to use your special talents and unique abilities to their fullest,

YOU JUST HAVEN'T SHOWN UP!

**Showing Up is
POSITIVE ACTION.**

**It's a proactive strategy for
YOUR LIFE.**

It is that first important step that you must take to move beyond ...

just wishing
for great things to happen,

just hoping
for what you want and need,

just dreaming
about success!

Success – in every aspect of your life – begins when you come face to face with opportunities and you are totally, completely there.

Those who show up to GO FOR IT are the people most likely to GET IT.

~ Nicole Schoychid

So, make a commitment to

SHOW UP
MORE OFTEN!

Do your very best to BE THERE for every success opportunity you are given.

You'll stand a better chance of accomplishing your initial goal

AND

Additional golden opportunities will be more likely to come your way!

Think about what would
happen if tomorrow –

in every aspect of your professional
and personal life –

you made a special effort
to be there ...

100% PHYSICALLY MENTALLY EMOTIONALLY

The positive outcomes are limitless for you – and for others connected to you and your life.

Try it!

Do it!

REPEAT IT AGAIN AND AGAIN!

The way to get started is to quit talking and begin doing.

~ Walt Disney

GO FOR THE GOLD

SUIT UP

**Always be ready
to ACHIEVE**

You cannot climb the ladder of success dressed in the costume of failure.

~ Zig Ziglar

Whatever you are doing, whatever challenges you face, whatever **"Gold"** you are seeking, **you must SHOW UP and then ...**

SUIT UP
FOR SUCCESS.

Suiting up is less about what you wear and more about how you prepare.

One of the best and clearest ways to understand the SUIT UP component of success is through a sports analogy.

Think about successful teams or individual athletes – those who excel in their fields of endeavor.

What do they do to SUIT UP?

Certainly there's the obvious – they put on some type of uniform or special gear appropriate for the event. But that's a very small part of what they do. For these people,

SUITING UP means being ready to achieve.

It means preparing themselves to achieve success. And that entails a lot more than merely getting dressed.

Here's what successful athletes do to SUIT UP:

- ✓ They **hone their skills and abilities** through never-ending practice.

- ✓ They **stay in top physical condition** by eating well, resting well, and exercising.

- ✓ They **study and learn from the best** in their fields.

- ✓ They **acquire and use a vast array of tools and technologies** to compete effectively.

- ✓ They **analyze what they're up against** — familiarizing themselves with upcoming challenges and studying their competition.

✓ They **have a clear picture of their desired end-state** ... what they want to accomplish.

✓ They **formulate game plans**, strategies, and contingencies for achieving those ends.

✓ They **accept full responsibility** for their actions and performance.

✓ They **use setbacks as learning opportunities** to help them improve and grow.

and ...

✓ They "energize" themselves and their colleagues – bringing their emotions and self-confidence to high levels of **CAN DO / WILL DO determination.**

That's what high
achievers do.

**That's what YOU
need to do!**

Action is the foundational key to all success.

~ Pablo Picasso

What SUITING UP looks like ...

If you embrace continuous learning to enhance your skills, knowledge, and relationships,

YOU ARE SUITING UP!

If you start your day focused and determined to tackle your most important tasks,

YOU ARE SUITING UP!

If you stay informed about what's happening in your organization, your industry, your family, and your community,

YOU ARE SUITING UP!

If you have specific goals and concrete plans to accomplish those goals,

YOU ARE SUITING UP!

If you have contingency plans to deal with setbacks and unexpected occurrences,

YOU ARE SUITING UP!

If you have confidence in yourself and the drive to do what needs to be done,

YOU ARE SUITING UP!

If you are dedicated to achieving success while helping others do the same,

YOU *REALLY* ARE SUITING UP!

Positive things come to you when you're fully prepared and ready for them.

But there is a "catch" …

SUITING UP takes effort!

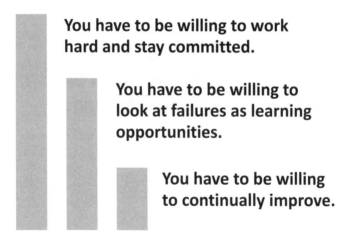

You have to be willing to work
hard and stay committed.

You have to be willing to
look at failures as learning
opportunities.

You have to be willing
to continually improve.

In order to succeed,
your desire for
success should be
greater than your
fear of failure.

~ Bill Cosby

In the real world, great achievements rarely just happen by chance. In fact, they rarely "just happen" at all.

Instead, they are **created** and **built** by people who *make them happen* ... people who

SHOW UP
Ready for ACTION

SUIT UP
Fully Prepared to ACHIEVE

Are you willing
to SHOW UP and SUIT UP?

Are you committed
to SHOWING UP and SUITING UP?

If so, you are ready to ...

GO FOR THE GOLD

and
Achieve Meaningful
and Lasting SUCCESS

So, exactly what is "GOLD"?

GOLD is something of great value and synonymous with success.

GOLD is diverse. It comes in many forms, shapes and sizes.

GOLD is precious and increases in value over time.

GOLD must be "mined." You have to work to obtain it.

more importantly ...

GOLD **is a standard** and exemplifies the pinnacle of quality ... the height of achievement ... the best of the best.

SUCCESS needs to become *your* "GOLD STANDARD."

Gold is not just given to you ... it's something of value that requires action and must be earned.

GOLD represents successes of every kind:

- Personal and professional achievement
- Helping your organization and your colleagues succeed
- Living with integrity
- Being a role model for others
- Demonstrating respect and responsibility
- Staying on top of marketplace trends and technology advances
- Leaving a positive legacy

And many other life examples.

But sometimes ...

GOING FOR THE GOLD can be a conflicting exercise.

There are, for example, only 1,440 minutes in each day. So, devoting all your time to just one success goal can hamper your ability to achieve other important personal and professional goals.

That's why you need

BALANCE that ensures you ...

◾ Attain results with integrity

◾ Deal with immediate needs without sacrificing long-term objectives

◾ Devote time to <u>ALL</u> of the important aspects of your personal and professional life

Lots of important goals require your time, but not all can receive your attention at the exact same moment.

Be sure to consistently evaluate your goals and the time you're devoting to each – so that nothing that's important gets shortchanged.

I believe that being successful means having a balance of success stories across the many areas of your life. You can't truly be considered successful in your business life if your home life is in shambles.

~ Zig Ziglar

Unbalanced success is really

FOOL'S GOLD –

the type of singular success that seems
all bright and shiny but is loaded with

"BUTS"

that often lead to very negative
long-term outcomes, like ...

- Having a very successful career,
  BUT neglecting your family in the process

- Getting that promotion you want,
  BUT leaving your former organization
  in total disarray

- Winning the championship game,
  BUT having your team take unethical
  "shortcuts" to achieve success

- Increasing your short-term profits,
  BUT compromising your long-term
  customer relationships

Don't be *fooled* into chasing

FOOL'S GOLD

and the "BUTS" that come with it.

Instead, concentrate your energy
and skills on producing

REAL GOLD

that is balanced, precious, and
increases in value over time.

You see ...

If you obtain career success and also achieve success in your personal life,

YOU'VE PRODUCED REAL GOLD!

If you increase productivity while also increasing the quality of your products and services,

YOU'VE PRODUCED REAL GOLD!

If you go "the extra mile" to satisfy your customers while also helping your coworkers succeed,

YOU'VE PRODUCED REAL GOLD!

If you are healthy in mind, body, and spirit,

YOU'VE PRODUCED REAL GOLD!

If you are the type of performer whom others admire and are motivated to emulate,

YOU'VE PRODUCED REAL GOLD!

If you achieve results with commitment, compassion, and integrity,

YOU'VE DEFINITELY PRODUCED
REAL GOLD!

GOING FOR THE GOLD
also requires continuous improvement and
ALWAYS REACHING HIGHER!

Here's an experiment for you to try:

Raise your right arm and hold your hand up as high as you can. Go ahead – give it a try.

Got it?

Now, this time try to hold your hand up just a little bit higher – even if it's only a fraction of an inch. Really stretch.

Could you do it? Most people can.

Now, ask yourself (and perhaps others):

How can I get my hand up even higher?

Let your creative juices flow!

Remove your "can't do" boundaries!

Take a few moments to stretch your mind with ideas like ...

- Stand on a chair or table

- Stretch your arm and jump up at the same time

- Make a human pyramid with you at the top

- Go to the top of the stairs

- Go to the roof of your building

- Rent a helicopter or airplane and ...

OKAY, YOU GET THE POINT.

In today's highly competitive
and ever-changing world,

GOING FOR THE GOLD

requires:

Creativity and Continuous Improvement

✓ **Every day**

✓ **In every situation**

✓ **With every goal you and
your organization have.**

The backbone of success is ... hard work, determination, good planning, and perseverance.

~ Mia Hamm

So, how can you achieve success when it comes to ...

Your job?

Your career?

Your family?

Your community?

Your team?

Your organization?

YOUR LIFE?

You now have the answer!

SHOW UP

Stop Dreaming and Start DOING!

**BE THERE Physically, Mentally
and Emotionally.**

**Footprints on the path
of life are not made
by those sitting down.**

~ Erika Westmoreland

SUIT UP

Always Be Ready to ACHIEVE!

Prepare Yourself for Success Opportunities.

Some people merely dream of success while others work hard, stay committed, and consistently improve to achieve their goals.

~ Steve Ventura

GO FOR THE GOLD

Achieve Meaningful and Lasting Success.

Give It All You've Got!

For true success, ask yourself ...
Why not? Why not Me?
Why not NOW?

~ James Allen

You're off to
great places!
Today is your day!
Your mountain
is waiting, So ...
get on your way!

~ Dr. Seuss

GO FOR THE GOLD

CLOSING THOUGHTS

As human beings, we all are special and unique.

We have different faces, personalities, interests, and desires ... different motivations ... different bodies, minds, and spirits. But we also share just as many similarities as we exhibit differences. And one of those things we all have in common is the desire to be truly SUCCESSFUL – in our careers and our relationships ... at work and away from the job.

By nature, we all are dream chasers.

We're all on the same never-ending quest to achieve meaningful and lasting success.

We're all prospectors searching for our brand of GOLD.

And while that GOLD we seek may be somewhat different for each of us, the behaviors necessary to "mine" it – to achieve our goals – are the same for ALL of us.

Identifying those behaviors – the DOING requirements for success – is what this book, this important message, is all about.

Greater success than you have ever known is waiting just around the corner.

Don't wait another minute. Don't waste another second. Only you can make it happen. Be there. Be ready. Find your balance. Give it all you've got.

SHOW UP. SUIT UP.

Now,
GO FOR THE
GOLD!

ACTION ITEMS

Always bear in mind that your own resolution to succeed is more important than any one thing.

~ Abraham Lincoln

How I Can GO FOR THE GOLD

1. Fully capture these important messages by reading this book multiple times.

(Add more below.)

_____

_____

_____

_____

_____

_____

_____

_____

_____

_____

_____

_____

_____

_____

_____

_____

_____

_____

Don't stop here – add more on a regular basis.

And remember ...

Always GO FOR THE GOLD!

10-*Plus* Ways to
Turn This Information into ACTION

1. Add a "Go for the Gold" topic to the agendas of future meetings and discussions.

2. Share these powerful messages with your family, friends, and coworkers.

3. Give GO FOR THE GOLD to new employees as a welcoming gift.

4. Incorporate these messages into leadership and employee development activities.

5. Use "Go for the Gold" as a slogan to support organizational goals.

6. Give **GO FOR THE GOLD** to team members to mark and celebrate a special occasion.

7. Use "Go for the Gold" as a motivational "kick-off" message when launching new projects or initiatives.

8. Give **GO FOR THE GOLD** as recognition for employee and coworker achievements and contributions.

9. Use **GO FOR THE GOLD** as a meeting or conference resource to support your business objective.

10. Make "Go for the Gold" your standard for excellence and achievement.

Add additional WAYS below:

_____

_____

_____

_____

_____

_____

_____

_____

_____

_____

Powerful Reminders About
GOING FOR THE GOLD

There are no shortcuts to any place worth going.
~ Beverly Sills

At one point in your life you either have the thing you want or the reasons why you don't.
~ Andy Roddick

Too many people go through life
waiting for things to happen
instead of making them happen.
~ Sasha Azevedo

**I find that the harder I work,
the more luck I seem to have.**
~ Thomas Jefferson

Ability may get you to the top, but
it takes character to keep you there.
~ John Wooden

Success is liking yourself,
liking what you do,
and liking how you do it.
~ Maya Angelou

When love and determination
work together,
expect a masterpiece.
~ Tamz

The only place you find success before work is in the dictionary.
~ May V. Smith

The elevator to success is out of order.
You'll have to use the stairs ...
one step at a time.
~ Joe Girard

Don't let negative and toxic people rent space in your head. Raise the rent and kick them out!
~ Robert Tew

Success is more permanent when you achieve
it without destroying your principles.
~ Walter Cronkite

**Never give up and always keep fighting,
because though times may be tough,
the sacrifices do pay off, so just
keep pushing towards your dream.**
~ Gabby Douglas
(Olympic GOLD medalist)

If your ship doesn't come in,
swim out to meet it.
~ Jonathan Winters

GO FOR THE GOLD

About the Author

ERIC HARVEY, founder of **Walk The Talk** and **Go for the Gold,** is a consultant, entrepreneur, and leading expert on high-achieving individuals and organizations. His 25 books have sold millions of copies worldwide and include the bestsellers *WALK THE TALK*, *The Leadership Secrets of Santa Claus*, and *Ethics4Everyone*.

Eric devotes his time to consulting, writing, and family — which includes his wife, Nancy; two daughters, Erika and Nicole, who work at Walk The Talk; and his five grandchildren who, as Eric says, "teach me the meaning and purpose of going for the gold every day."

GO FOR THE GOLD by Eric Harvey

1–99 copies	$10.95 each
100–499 copies	$9.95 each

Special pricing available for orders over 500 copies: Call 888.822.9255

Also available as an e-book

GO FOR THE GOLD DVD

The powerful movie that motivates groups of all types and sizes to achieve meaningful and lasting success.

To view this movie and learn about GO FOR THE GOLD support resources, visit walkthetalk.com and click on the GO FOR THE GOLD icon.

$295.00

Three easy ways to order
GO FOR THE GOLD Resources

online   **walkthetalk.com**

---

phone   **888.822.9255** (toll-free)
or 972.899.8300
Monday through Friday
8:30 a.m. – 5:00 p.m. Central

---

fax   **972.899.9291**

Stay connected with GO FOR THE GOLD

 Visit **walkthetalk.com** and click on the
GO FOR THE GOLD icon to learn about
new support resources and special offers.

 Share your suggestions and GO FOR THE GOLD
success stories.

    email   gold@walkthetalk.com

    mail   GO FOR THE GOLD
           1100 Parker Square, Suite 250
           Flower Mound, TX 75028

We'd love to hear how GO FOR THE GOLD
is making a positive difference for you and
your organization!

GO FOR THE GOLD